TIPS

Teaching Music to Special Learners

TIPS

Teaching Music to Special Learners

Compiled by
Gail Schaberg

MENC Special Learners Chair

MENC
The National Association for Music Education

1806 Robert Fulton Drive
Reston, Virginia 20191-4348

Printed in the United States of America
ISBN 0-940796-56-2

Table of Contents

Foreword

MENC: The National Association for Music Education has created the TIPS series to provide music educators with a variety of ideas on a wide range of practical subjects. Each TIPS booklet is a compilation of methods, ideas, and suggestions that have been successful in the music classroom. MENC has designed this quick-reference series to be used as a starting point for creating and adapting projects for your particular situation.

Sensory Stimulation and Self-Concept

Children need training to make the best use of their five senses. Visual, auditory, and tactile or kinesthetic senses are of greatest concern in the music class. The following TIPS can help children improve their understanding and awareness of these sensations, can suggest acceptable ways of developing them, and can help develop a more positive self-concept for special learners who have low self-esteem.

Arrange students as partners, seated or standing back to back, to help young children develop greater sensory awareness and improve their ability to move rhythmically and respond to directions; to develop breathing, phrasing, and speech skills; and to develop auditory acuity. Have children imitate or echo each other's breathing sounds and movements. The leader breathes in patterns, and the other child imitates. The patterns can be fast (huffing and puffing as if running), slow (deep breathing, snoring, and yawning), or with pitch (humming, whistling, bird calls, and animal sounds, all of which can help students pronounce vowels and consonants).

With students facing each other, one child places a hand on the the other child's throat or cheek to feel the vibrations. Students should feel the difference among whispering, speaking loud, and singing. This exercise helps students understand the source of the human voice and how a singing tone is produced. These exercises could be used to help with speech impairments, delayed speech, or to develop the singing voice.

Adapted from Carol Guymer, "Special Spectrum," *North Dakota Music Educator*, December 1984, 11-12.

* * *

Make a mystery box by taking a small box with a lid and placing a mirror face up on the bottom. Tell the group, "The best thing in the whole world is inside the box." Intensify the mystery of the box by saying that whoever looks in the box must keep what they see a secret. At the end of a class, reinforce appropriate behavior by allowing a student to look into the box. This reward is recommended as a tool for building self-esteem for people of all ages. Use it sparingly to build suspense.

* * *

Use a song like "Names Have Rhythm" (see figure 1) that incorporates students' names. After singing the song, several children take turns saying their names rhythmically while playing a tambourine or other instrument. Hearing their name, saying their name, and playing the rhythm that represents their name gives students individual recognition, momentarily focuses attention, and helps individual children feel important.

Figure 1

* * *

Develop listening skills by filling pairs of boxes or small cans (such as plastic 35mm film containers) with various objects that make sounds (for example, salt, nails, or marbles). Have students select a container, shake it, and listen and then shake the others until a match is found. Have students continue until pairs for all the containers have been found. This activity is recommended for most populations, including educable and trainable mentally retarded students.

* * *

Set up five stations in the classroom and include a variety of sound producers in each. For example:

Station 1: metal objects (keys, spoons, triangles, cymbals, and pan covers)

Station 2: wooden objects (pencils, sticks, wooden bowls, and logs)
Station 3: paper items (cups, plates, cardboard, crumbled paper, and torn paper)
Station 4: plastic objects (cups, spoons, cartons, and ice cream containers)
Station 5: body sounds (claps, taps, snaps, vocal sounds, patschen [slapping hands on thighs], and whistles)

Organize the class into five groups. Each group should experiment with its station's sounds. After group members have a chance to practice, ask them to create a rhythm to fit some music. Put several sound station creations together to make a "symphony," and select a student conductor to direct it. Expand the lesson by mapping the sounds on paper, giving each student a turn at conducting and arranging, and using different meters and styles in the selected music accompaniment. Have students rotate to different stations. You might want to give a prize to the most creative group.

Adapted from Joan Muckenhirn-Morton and Carol Guymer, "Special Spectrum," *North Dakota Music Educator,* May 1985, 24.

* * *

Give students hats to wear. The teacher sings the following song, naming both the person with the hat and the person to whom it will be passed. When hearing the name of the next person, the student with the hat takes it off and passes it to that person. The student whose name is sung should make eye contact with the teacher. The song continues until everyone has had a turn.

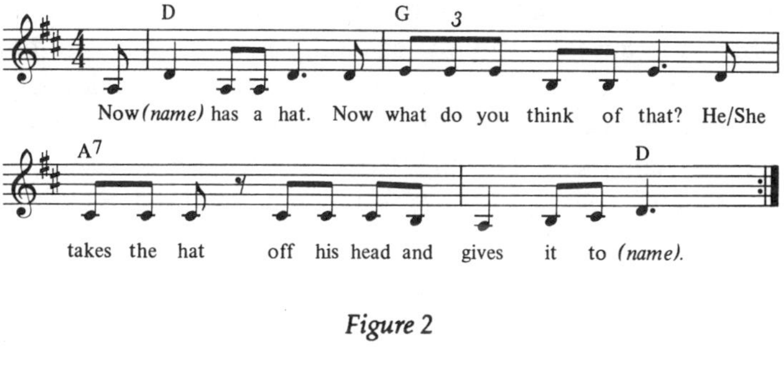

Figure 2

Use scarves or free-flowing materials to help students express grace, tempo change, and style and to allow "dancing" by some students who would not normally be able to do it. Scarves can be used to express beauty and poise and help create a lovely experience for all. Students can also use large, brightly colored balls while moving to music. Children can imitate the teacher's movement or make up their own movements. Phrases and rhythmic patterns can be recognized in the movement of the balls, and the activity can be done while standing or sitting. This activity is good for most students, especially those with behavior disorders and physical disabilities.

* * *

Young children have fun with activities they can move to and that help them identify various body parts. Have students make believe they are taking a bath. You will need washcloths and recordings such as "Splish Splash" by Bobby Darin, "Rubber Duckie" from Sesame Street, or any lively instrumental selection. Students hold washcloths (or pretend they are holding them) and receive either visual or aural cues from the teacher regarding where to "wash." People of all ages have fun participating in this activity.

* * *

Children love to play "hot potato"; this game can be used to reinforce accents in music and a spirit of teamwork in keeping the ball moving. Have the students sit in a circle. Play music that is in 3/4 time, and instruct the students to pass the ball to the person on their right on the first beat and count on beats two and three (pass, two, three, pass, two, three). One variation is to add one or more balls. Another variation is to instruct children that when the music stops, whoever is holding the ball is out of the game. Continue until one student is left as the winner. This game creates excitement and reinforces strong rhythmic beats. It is useful for learning-disabled and educable mentally retarded persons.

Have each student choose a rhythm instrument. When the teacher is playing a guitar or other instrument, the students are to play; when the music stops, they are to stop. If all students stop when they should, the teacher continues the activity. If a student continues playing after the music stops, the teacher takes away the instrument and continues the activity, but that student remains in the activity by pretending he or she is still playing the instrument. Tell the students that the removal of instruments is not a punishment but merely part of the game. The last person to have an instrument is the winner. This activity helps students sharpen listening skills and learn how to win and lose gracefully.

* * *

Although music series books often are too difficult for special learners to read, they can learn the words, rhythms, and movements of the music by rote and by mapping (diagraming the contour of a melody). When students make their own songbooks, they are working toward achievement of several goals: development of coordinated movement of arms and hands, development of powers of thought and recognition, and development of imagination. Songs and listening pieces with story lines are appropriate, such as "This Old Man," "There Was an Old Lady Who Swallowed a Fly," and "This Land Is Your Land."

* * *

Have students make an alphabet or number songbook by pasting felt cutouts on a piece of fabric such as corduroy, felt, or burlap. These books are especially meaningful for twelve- to twenty-one-year-old mentally retarded students who wish to have music and activities that are more in keeping with their young adult world. The following songs are appropriate: "Big Rock Candy Mountain" (Silver Burdett and Ginn), "Joy to the World" (the pop version by Silver Burdett and Ginn), "Sing a Rainbow" (Macmillan), "America the Beautiful," and "Sounds of Silence" (Eclectic Music Company).

Adapted from Carol Guymer, "Special Spectrum," *North Dakota Music Educator*, October, 1984, 8.

* * *

Exceptionalities

Every TIP, suggestion, or activity that a teacher considers or uses should be adapted to the needs of the child or class involved. Some TIPS seem especially well suited to a particular type of disability and have been listed in this section under the following categories: physical disabilities, behavior disorders, mental retardation, visual impairments, hearing impairments, communication disorders, and gifted and talented.

Physical Disabilities

This category includes a wide spectrum of problems from mild to severe, a single disability or a combination of impairments, an impairment from birth or one acquired at a later time, and a variety of causes and types. Among these are orthopedic impairments (those affecting the bones, muscles, and limbs); neurological impairments (those involving the use or feeling of certain body parts); and other health problems, both permanent and temporary, that might affect the way a child functions in a music class.

* * *

To help the mainstreaming process, music teachers are trying to meet each child's needs in the music classroom. Unfortunately, music educators who are unfamiliar with certain illnesses and handicaps are sometimes reluctant to recommend instrumental or vocal instruction because they fear that the exertion and rigor of practice may have adverse effects on the children. With some understanding of the physical requirements of performance and the basic nature of the physical problem, however, music teachers can open up an aesthetic world that has been denied for handicapped students. Some helpful information for music educators is found in the book *Guide to the Selection of Musical Instruments with Respect to Physical Ability and Disability* by Barbara Elliott.

Adapted from Suzanne B. Hanser, "Resources for Physically Handicapped Musicians," *California Music Educators Association News,* February-March 1985, 7.

* * *

Play some lively music that motivates children to move. When the music stops, the children should freeze. This game can be played either standing or sitting, and all ages love it. It is a good activity for enhancing motor coordination.

* * *

Behavior Disorders

Children with these disorders behave in extreme, chronic, and excessive ways that do not conform to the social expectations of their culture. They usually do not relate well to others, are unhappy individuals, do not respond to normal teaching methods, and are probably the greatest cause for concern in the classroom. Behavior disorders range from lashing out and aggression toward others to extreme withdrawal.

* * *

The following are some guidelines for working effectively with students who have emotional handicaps: (1) Encourage maximum musical involvement and use minimal verbal instruction, (2) provide room for individual expression within a carefully structured class, (3) ensure a successful musical product (performance) at the conclusion of each class, (4) use improvisation or composition to stimulate creative expression, and (5) reward appropriate behavior or interaction with specific music privileges (such as choosing songs for the class to sing, listening to a favorite recording, being a group leader, or getting the first choice of instruments to play).

Adapted from Suzanne B. Hanser, "Music with Emotionally Disturbed Children," *California Music Educators Association News,* September-October, 1985, 9.

To avoid having students punch, shove, or kick each other when they are doing creative movement, you need to teach spatial awareness. Here are several suggestions. Make a circle and sing these words to the tune of "Brother John":

> Make a circle, make a circle
> Make it round, make it round
> Make a circle, make a circle
> Before you sit down (or "And don't sit down")

Have children move to the right or to the left (as designated by the leader) to a beat from a piano, a drum, or a shaker. When the music stops, clap once, turn, and go the other way. This is a good way to teach phrases, rests, directions, and spatial awareness.

Accompanied by a drum, some children move to the center and back, while others move to the outside of the circle with hops and skips. All move to the beat of the instrument.

* * *

Have the children measure the spaces in front of them, beside them, and behind them. Tell them that these areas are their spaces and no one else can be in them.

When the students have achieved good spatial awareness skills, they can perform movement activities with scarves, streamers, or rhythm instruments to accompany poems and musical selections such as *Danse macabre*, the *Nutcracker Suite*, *Carnival of the Animals*, or *Star Wars*.

Adapted from Carol Guymer, "Special Spectrum," *North Dakota Music Educator*, December 1987, 10.

* * *

Using a five-piece drum set can help students release tension, keep rhythm, and feel important—all at the same time. If children come to music class bursting with energy, start with a familiar song accompanied by the drums. Children will be much more responsive than if they sing unaccompanied.

Use physical exercises when your students are tense and unable to concentrate. Put on a recording of slow, gentle music to help create a relaxed mood. Have children exercise on padded mats (if possible) to ensure their safety. The following are some exercises that can be used:

1. Tell children to stretch out tall and wide, then collapse or flop over. Repeat several times.

2. Have them sit on the floor, hold their knees, and roll around like balls.

3. Instruct students to slowly wave scarves or streamers in patterns in the air; this helps them take their minds off themselves.

4. Tell children to stand in place and slowly roll their heads in one direction and then the other; to raise one shoulder, then the other; and to roll their shoulders alternately in little circles.

5. Have pairs of children face each other; one child makes slow movements, and the other tries to imitate each movement as a "reflection" in a mirror. The teacher (or a student) also can create the movements while all others try to imitate.

6. Tell children to act out various animals that move slowly.

7. Use your imagination and try other relaxing exercises.

* * *

Mental Retardation

Mentally retarded children function below average intellectually and are socially immature and unable to function independently and responsibly. They are usually placed in special classes for educable mentally handicapped or trainable mentally handicapped students. Recently, children who have been labeled profoundly handicapped have also been enrolled in the public schools. It is important to know that all of these children can learn within certain limitations, although at a slower rate, if proper educational programs and teaching methods are used. Their skills are usually weak in all areas.

A favorite game for mentally handicapped students is the "car game." Have students move about the room "driving" make-believe cars, buses, sports cars, and vans to rhythmic beats of an instrument and made-up songs. With trainable mentally handicapped students, use songs such as as "Mulberry Bush" ("This is the way to drive my van . . ."), "When I was a drummer" ("Oh, when I was a taxi . . ."), and "Goin' for a Ride" from Sesame Street. Students move and stop on green and red signals the teacher has made. Students' outstretched arms are used as "headlights." The learnings include (1) rhythm, beat, tempo, and rests ("stop signs"); (2) vocal development (imitating the gears); (3) timbre and texture of sounds; and (4) self-discipline and control in an active group involvement.

Adapted from Jeanette Hinds and Carol Guymer, "Special Spectrum," *North Dakota Music Educator*, May 1987, 12-13.

* * *

Use brightly colored visual aids to enhance the music for profoundly handicapped students, such as streamers, scarves, balloons, puppets, parachutes, cutouts, pictures, instruments, bubbles, mirrors, simple costumes, or colored slides.

* * *

Allow students with profound mental and multiple handicaps to make choices in their activities. For example, allow students to choose an instrument, grasp it, and play it, with or without assistance, to the beat of a lively recording such as "The Fifth of Beethoven." Or, if the activity is waving streamers, let them choose which of two colors they prefer rather than just giving them one.

* * *

Educable mentally handicapped (EMH) children can successfully learn music skills in an instrumental music program. These children are ready, willing, and often able to learn. The following guidelines are intended to help teachers introduce instrumental music instruction to EMH children.

1. The four traditional stages of instruction are recruitment, individual instruction, group instruction, and performance. These techniques can be used with EMH children if some modifications are made: an initial period of individual instruction, an emphasis on playing by ear, and the use of ikonic notation (fingerings placed under the notes or a system of symbols, note names, or keys to aid note recognition).

2. There must be cooperation among parents, music specialists, classroom teachers, and supportive personnel.

3. Teachers must teach students how to care for and maintain their instruments.

4. Students must receive a gradual introduction to group ensemble performance.

5. Every phase of instruction should contain reinforcement techniques coupled with planned experiences in success.

Adapted from Paul E. Rosene, "Instrumental Music . . . A Success Opportunity," *Music Educators Journal,* 68, no. 8, April 1982, 37-39; and Paul E. Rosene, "Musical Insights for the Exceptional Child," *Illinois Music Educator,* Summer 1979, 4-7.

* * *

Trainable mentally handicapped students can make puppets and use them to learn songs, vocabulary words, days of the week, seasons, song history, and, most important, self-control and self-worth. The students gain an astonishing amount of learning and a product that can be taken home and shared with their families. When children make puppets, those creations become extensions of their personalities; they will dance, sing, act, play parts, and willingly learn skills that they either would not ordinarily do by themselves or could not do themselves if they are confined to wheelchairs. Puppets can be made from fingers (faces painted on fingers), potatoes, paper bags, paper towels, magazine pictures, or sticks (paint stirrers, pencils, or clothespins).

* * *

Learning Disabilities

This is one of the most controversial and difficult disabilities to define. A discrepancy between a child's potential to achieve and what he actually does achieve is readily apparent, meaning that a child with average or above-average intelligence is achieving significantly below that level. There are usually difficulties in reading, writing, language, or arithmetic, and the child exhibits such characteristics as hyperactivity, attention disorders, perceptual-motor problems, and impulsiveness.

* * *

Many learning-disabled students are unable to stay in their own spaces, especially in a large area such as an auditorium or gymnasium. You can establish guidelines by placing stickers on the floor where each student is to sit or by outlining an area with masking tape. Have students sit on rug samples or hula hoops, or outline a small area on the floor (such as a square or circle) with masking tape.

* * *

To help learning-disabled students memorize a song in a short time, color code the notes. Put a permanent color code on a wall chart, and introduce a new thinking game called "play that picture." All the boxes (notes) are two inches high, and they do not move up and down but are placed beside each other (the colors replace the staff). This technique is not intended to teach children to read music; it is a way to stimulate brain processes, and it makes a pretty bulletin board. Colors could be brown (middle C), yellow (D), purple (E), black (F), green (G), orange (A), blue (B), red (C), blue-green (D), red-violet (E), yellow-green (F), and pink (G).

Adapted from Cak Marshall, "Elementary Fun Page," *Pennsylvania Music Educators News*, March 1987, 17.

* * *

Visual Impairments

In educational terms, visual impairments include blindness (learning and reading through senses other than vision, principally by braille and listening) and low vision (using vision for learning, but needing large-print materials). Visually impaired students are usually found in regular classrooms, but they may need special materials or teaching techniques.

* * *

To help students who are visually impaired, decorate the classroom by tacking large sheets of wallpaper on the wall. Print some favorite songs on the paper using large letters. Enlarge music notation symbols by using transparencies and an overhead projector to give students a large visual field for greater "right brain" processing.

* * *

Select popular songs with which visually impaired children may be familiar. Teach basic dance steps (for example, slow drag and modified swing), and have students dance with you to the music until they gain confidence. Emphasize strong and weak beats during the dance. This activity establishes social skills that can be used later and reinforces gross motor development (large muscle groups). You can also teach the concepts of phrasing and form during these activities by grouping a certain number of foot patterns into a phrase and by changing patterns or direction for each phrase or section of the song.

* * *

Teach a common, everyday task to a group of blindfolded students so they can gain a better understanding of those who are visually impaired. When teaching blindfolded children, one must rethink lessons in greater detail and explain them more clearly than in other lessons. Although tactile cues are available to these learners, the inability to rely on visual aids creates a need for concise and explicit instruction.

Adapted from Carol A. Prickett, "Blind Musicians . . . Not Just a Fairy Tale," *Ala Breve*, December 1986, 6.

Some children have difficulty with the concept of left and right, which they need for some dances or action songs. Have them hold up both thumbs and index fingers (palms down) to see which hand forms the letter "L" (for "left"). A red dot or a piece of tape can also be placed on the right hand, knee, or foot to indicate the right one.

* * *

When addressing a visually impaired person in a group, always address him or her by name. Take the time to make sure that the person can perceive your responses.

* * *

Ensure the safety of students with visual impairments by informing them of rearranged furniture or doors left ajar. Although sighted people often feel self-conscious about using words such as "see," "looks like," or "watch," those with severe visual handicaps use these terms frequently.

* * *

Hearing Impairments

Both deafness and poor hearing are included in this category, and both involve difficulty in hearing and understanding speech. The deaf child, even with a hearing aid, will not be able to comprehend speech through hearing alone. The hard-of-hearing child may be able to understand speech with a hearing aid, but speech and language skills will be somewhat deficient. Almost all hearing impairments are also combined with communication impairments, and in most instances they necessitate special training. Most children are not totally deaf, and they have at least some ability to hear certain sounds.

* * *

Use signs when singing to achieve heightened communication between normal-hearing and hearing-impaired children. Normal-hearing children learn another language, and hearing-impaired children gain a better understanding of music. This communication can only occur if sign language is used properly.

Adapted from Alice-Ann Darrow, "Exploring the Arts of Sign and Song," *Music Educators Journal*, 74, no. 1, September 1987, 35.

* * *

Picture cards that illustrate verses or words to songs help students who are hearing impaired or mentally retarded learn or recall songs such as "Old MacDonald," "B-I-N-G-O," "The Twelve Days of Christmas," "Do-Re-Mi," and "My Aunt Came Back."

* * *

If you teach students with hearing impairments, you must learn the proper use of hearing aids and some basic sign language. Exaggerated sign language movements look like dance gestures and can be aesthetically pleasing. Provide visual models of rhythmic and melodic patterns with charts and demonstrations. These patterns do not have to be traditional notation; Kodály pictorial notation of rhythms are effective with young hearing-impaired children who do not yet know music notation.

Provide hand-over-hand prompts by placing your hand on the student's hand and guiding it so the child gains a kinesthetic sense or understanding of the pattern. Reduce the difficulty or the amount of information to be learned using a simple rhythmic pattern or a short one that repeats. Orff ostinati are perfect for this activity.

Adapted from Kate Gfeller, "Adapting Orff Materials for the Handicapped Child: Part II—Communication," *Iowa Music Educator*, September 1986, 21-22.

* * *

Communication Disorders

The process of communication involves a message, a sender, and a receiver. Problems may occur in transmitting the message (expressive language) or in receiving or comprehending it (receptive language). In the classroom these problems may suggest impaired speech or language disorders (reading difficulties, other comprehension problems, a limited vocabulary, or incorrect use of the language).

* * *

Children with specific learning disabilities (also those with behavior disorders or mental retardation) sometimes have difficulty understanding the spoken language. There are many ways to communicate information to them using no words or very few words.

1. *Sign language.* This is a very useful skill. It is also helpful to learn a few key words to reinforce the spoken language. Learning to sign songs is a meaningful experience for all children; books are available to show how to sign some familiar songs (see Selected Readings).

2. *Imitation.* Before children can feel comfortable with creative movements, they need to learn a repertoire of moves. Have students imitate the teacher, and then have them express themselves or create their own movements.

3. *Sound cues.* Certain sounds or instrumental cues can be assigned a special meaning. The IV-I chord progression ("Amen") might mean that students should stop what they are doing or stop talking; a sudden drum beat or cymbal crash could indicate that children are to go to their seats; a slide whistle could be a cue to stand up or sit down.

4. *Gestures.* Kodály hand signs can be used to indicate various pitch levels; positive reinforcement can be given through a smile, the "okay" sign, a thumbs-up, a "bravo" gesture, or drawing a big heart with two fingers.

* * *

Music lessons that coordinate with other classroom activities provide enrichment in both areas. Vocabulary building is especially important for some students. Whenever possible, try to develop music activities around the academic subject matter taught in early elementary grades and in classes for educable mentally handicapped or trainable mentally handicapped students to reinforce classroom concepts.

Adapted from Carol Guymer, "Special Spectrum," *North Dakota Music Educator,* March 1987, 13.

Use puppets to work on speech problems. Students enjoy them; they forget their inhibitions and do not mind working on laborious speech drills.

* * *

Collect songs that include repetitions of various sounds. Use them with children who are involved in speech therapy to relieve the monotony of repetitious drill. You can find a number of familiar songs that emphasize a particular sound, but it is fun and easy to write your own. Remember to use the targeted sound in the initial, medial, and final positions of words. Tongue twisters are fun to put to music, and the children enjoy the challenge.

* * *

Gifted and Talented

Gifted and talented children are not included under the Education for All Handicapped Children Act (Public Law 94-142), but they frequently need a "special" education because they do not always respond to normal teaching methods. They are the students whom teachers hope to find in a music class so they can nurture and develop their unique gifts and talents.

* * *

Use the "mentor system" when working with gifted students. Older students paired with younger students as assistants or tutors can motivate and encourage the learners while reinforcing their own self-esteem.

* * *

There are two pitfalls in teaching gifted students. The first mistake involves a lowering of social standards. It is not unusual for teachers and parents to inadvertently encourage poor social interactions. Acceptance of displays of temper, boasting, condescension, or eccentric behavior as natural concomitants of superior abilities is detrimental to students. The second mistake is overcriticism. A person of exceptional academic or musical ability does not automatically possess exceptionally high self-esteem. Students who do not know when they have done something poorly probably cannot recognize when they have done quite well. The formula of giving four positive observations for every corrective comment should be used with all students.

Adapted from Carol Prickett, "Working with Gifted and Talented Students: The Pitfalls," *Ala Breve*, October 1987, 39.

* * *

Development of Skills and Concepts

The primary purpose of most music classes is to provide a basic music education that includes developing specific skills, broader understandings, and an appreciation for many types of music. The music class, however, is also an ideal setting for developing various other skills that handicapped children may lack. The following TIPS include suggestions for improving music skills and understandings as well as other abilities such as social skills and eye and hand coordination.

Music notation is one of the most difficult concepts for some mentally retarded and learning-disabled children to grasp. There are many ways to modify notation and decrease the amount of information presented so that these students can fully participate in the class.

1. Do not use staff lines. It also may not be necessary to use key signatures and time signatures. (A single number may be used to indicate the number of beats in a measure.)

2. Use bar lines to divide the music into measures and to distinguish patterns and groupings of notes.

3. Do not use rests when an instrument does not play for one or several measures; leave the space blank.

4. Color code single lines of rhythmic patterns for each instrument or voice, using bright and contrasting colors, so students can follow their colors when playing.

5. Color code melodic lines for each instrument.

6. Use shapes to represent the instruments (such as a triangle for that instrument, a circle for drums or tambourines, or crossed sticks for rhythm sticks), indicating each note or which instrument plays each line.

7. Show eighth notes as two small symbols occupying the same amount of space as a larger quarter-note symbol.

8. Align beats for the various parts, one under the other, so that the children can see which parts are playing simultaneously.

Intricate charts can be devised and understood by the children, but it takes careful, step-by-step practice for them to learn their parts. Begin with one part at a time, not all at once.

* * *

To keep classes energized, use special phrases to hold the attention of students. Phrases such as "Let me see your eyes," "Look here at the picture," and "See Randy's fingers" usually draw attention. Use of students' names and praise also helps pull the class together. Highlighting student successes is probably the most effective tool. "I am looking for the ones who do it right" is an attention-getting remark. Charts showing successful performers give concrete evidence of success. These suggestions work with students whose attention spans are short.

Adapted from Cecilia Schmitt, "New Ideas for Teaching the Handicapped," *Gopher Music Notes*, April 1987, 39.

* * *

One way to teach 6/8 time is to use half-inch graph paper. Represent notes in units of two blocks high (one inch) by one block wide (one-half inch). Each unit represents an eighth note in 6/8 time. (A quarter note is represented by two units, a half note by four units, and so forth.) By drawing the appropriate number of units for quarters, halves, dotted halves, and whole notes, you can notate rhythmic patterns in nearly any time signature. You can also include a color-coded chart to represent a melodic line. This technique is helpful for students who need concrete examples (see figure 3).

Adapted from Cak Marshall, "Elementary Fun Page," *Pennsylvania Music Educators News*, May 1987, 17.

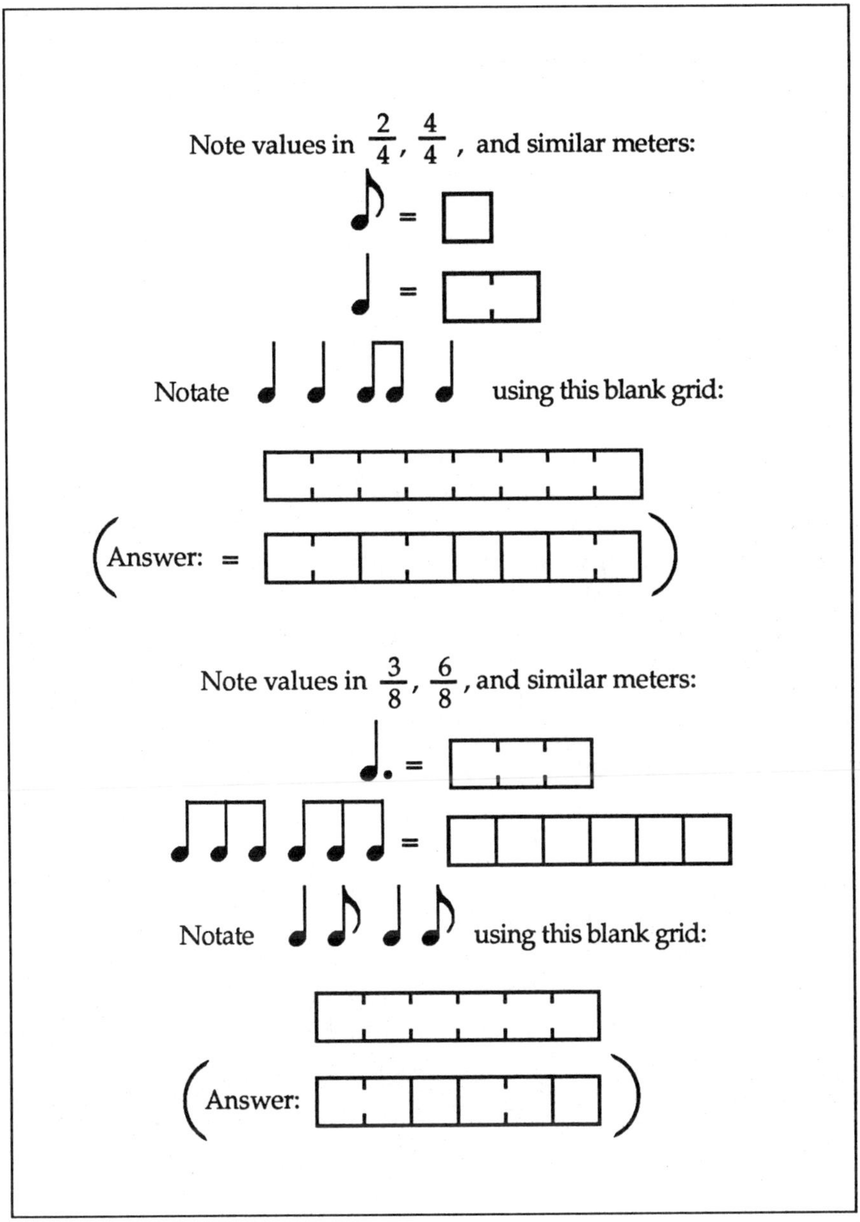
Note values in 2/4, 4/4, and similar meters:
Notate
using this blank grid:
Answer: =
Note values in 3/8, 6/8, and similar meters:
Notate
using this blank grid:
Answer:

Figure 3

Work on pitch both visually and aurally, using an eight-rung ladder, octave resonator bells, and cards with either the numbers one through eight or the names of the notes printed on them. (Cards should be large enough to fill in the spaces between the rungs.) Starting at the top, place a bell on each rung of the ladder in descending order (with the lowest note on the bottom rung), and affix the cards between the rungs. When teaching melodies, play the melody on the bells so students can see the rise and fall of the melody. Let the students take turns playing their melodies on the ladder.

* * *

Help special learners learn computer typing skills and reinforce the steady beat through a sequence of hand movements. Sing a familiar song that has ABA form. For the A section, have the child place both hands on the computer keyboard and play the steady beat to the song by pushing two keys simultaneously. For the B section, have the child play the steady beat with the right hand pushing one key (the child can also alternate left and right hands). Then go back to the A section, repeating the bilateral hand position. Print out what the child has played. The child can then sing the song again, tracing to the steady beat with his or her fingers the form created with letters.

* * *

Have children hold rhythm instruments and form a circle. While a recording is playing, you and the students should step to the beat. At a given signal a student performs the rhythmic pattern of his or her favorite flavor of ice cream on the instrument. For example:

"rasp- ber- ry ice cream"

All the children imitate the rhythm on their instruments, repeating the pattern four times. Everyone continues stepping in rhythm after the pattern has been played. Repeat this procedure until all students have had an opportunity to indicate their favorite flavor of ice cream. This activity helps improve movement, coordination, attention span, and sensitivity to rhythmic improvisation.

* * *

A very popular hands-on (actually feet-on) activity at a local Very Special Arts Festival was borrowed from Paul E. Rosene from Illinois. A number of rug samples obtained from local stores were placed on the hard, smooth floor, nap side down. One child stood on each rug sample and twisted to the lively beat of a recording played in the background. Some children needed help with this activity; others paired up with partners. Children in wheelchairs found this an especially exciting new way to be moved.

* * *

To help students experience the difference between loud and soft, teach them a simple two-line chant. After the chant is learned, divide students into two groups. On cue, one group chants pianissimo. The other group repeats the chant a little louder, and then the groups continue to alternate, louder and louder, four or five times until the volume reaches a small roar. Continue the chanting, reversing the dynamic level until the chant is pianissimo again.

* * *

An excellent way to teach sequence to students with mental handicaps is to tell a familiar story such as "The Three Bears." Mix up the sequence of the story and start with Goldilocks running down the stairs, frightened because the bears have found her in Little Bear's bed. Continue the out-of-sequence story by telling about Goldilocks eating the porridge, and finish by telling about her coming to the house and finding the bears gone. The class will enjoy retelling it correctly. They may wish to draw pictures and place them in order; these can be drawn on transparencies and used on the overhead projector. Make a "sound" picture by describing the following scenes with appropriate musical instruments: (1) bears blowing on the hot cereal, (2) bears going out of the door, (3) Goldilocks coming into the house, and so forth. Try mixing up the order of the scenes in the resulting sound story (a story told through instrumental sounds), putting it back into proper sequence. Another good story for this activity is "The Three Billy Goats Gruff"; use it to teach story sequence, tone colors, melodic sequences (each goat has a different melody line), and rhythmic sequences.

Adapted from Carol Guymer, "Special Spectrum," *North Dakota Music Educator*, October 1987, 22; December 1987, 9.

* * *

A unique, creative sound story and arts integration project can be achieved with this activity. Have the children decide what a little child would experience if he went to find a "round, red house with no doors and no windows and a star inside." The teacher guides the children's story by selecting instruments or environmental sounds they can use to create a story of a boy or girl's adventure in figuring out what is a "round, red house with no door and no windows, but a star inside" (answer: an apple). When the children have solved the mystery, the apple is sliced sideways (so everyone can see the "star"), and each child is given a slice of apple and a color of tempera paint. While the children say the story to themselves, have them dip the apple piece into the paint and stamp out a picture to the beat of the story until they have completed a picture. Some very interesting art works are created.

* * *

Create a maze by placing masking tape on the floor. Give all students rhythm instruments to play, and have them stand at different points along the maze. Blindfold one student and have him or her walk along the maze. The blindfolded student listens as the other students play on their instruments one at a time, starting at the beginning of the maze. The students can play a steady beat or some other practiced rhythmic pattern. The blindfolded student has to listen and locate the sound to complete the maze. Goals include listening and locating sound, trust, cooperation, and social skills.

* * *

Give a pair of lummi sticks (rhythm sticks) to each child, and play recorded music with an easily distinguishable beat. Create a series of challenging rhythm stick patterns to repeat and combine. Demonstrate the patterns for students, and instruct them to rehearse after each example. Gradually put all the patterns together, then rehearse and add recorded music. This activity is recommended for fourth- and fifth-grade students with educable mental handicaps, hearing impairments, or emotional handicaps.

* * *

Learn the song "Roll Over" with the following words: "There were ten in the bed and the little one said, 'Scoot over, scoot over.' So they all rolled over and [name] fell out. There were nine in the bed. . . ." Seat students side by side in chairs. Count all the students out loud, and have students count with you. If there are ten students, start singing the song with "ten in the bed." When the words "scoot over" are sung, the students scoot over to the next chair, and one student will lose his or her chair. (Practice the "scoot over" movement before you begin the activity.) Recount all students together out loud, and continue with the song. At the end, when one student is left in a chair, the "little one" says "good night." You can also add or subtract several children at a time.

* * *

The following activities are recommended for trainable mentally handicapped adolescents, but they can be adapted for other students.

- Listening: Play, hum, or tap a portion of a familiar melody. Students try to identify the "mystery tune."
- Vocal range: Help students explore how the voice moves up and down; imitate sounds of sirens, wind, ghosts, or owls.

- Pitch accuracy: Sing a song or phrase, and tell students to listen and "sing it in your mind." Hum beginning pitches before singing.
- Articulation: Ask students to (1) move their mouths, (2) whisper and speak words clearly after you (echo style), and (3) sing phrases staccato, marcato, and legato.

* * *

Students may be afraid to sing in front of others. An excellent way to help children get over their fears is to bring a "hose pipe" (actually a six-foot section of corrugated swimming pool hose) to class. Hold one end up to a child's ear, and sing a phrase or a couple of notes into the tube. Then move that end of the hose to the child's mouth, and have him or her echo what you just sang. As the children have fun, they forget to be embarrassed or afraid. This also is a good way to amplify sound for students with hearing impairments.

* * *

Students should be given time in every music class to listen to each other's singing. Ask for volunteers to sing a solo, or select students to sing alone or in groups. Do this every music class period. Always "tune up" before singing a song by giving children time to listen to the tuning note before they sing.

* * *

The word "zoom" (the sound of a jet) is an interesting sound to use with special learners. Begin at one pitch and slide up to a higher pitch, and have the children move their arms in an ascending motion.

* * *

Hum the starting note of a song. Humming promotes listening and lets the child find the note before the song starts. It is a quiet activity and sets the stage for the song.

Out-of-tune singers should be carefully placed in the room so the teacher can work easily with them. Place out-of-tune singers close to accurate singers, not at the back of the room or a far corner where they will learn little.

* * *

Pretend you are the engine of a train. Shuffle around the room, and stop at an out-of-tune singer's desk. If the child can successfully match your pitch, he or she can then "ride the train" by getting in line behind you. Move about the room, and pick up more and more children until all are a part of the "music train."

* * *

Have your students sing octave skips to help them match pitch. Many out-of-tune singers can correctly match large intervals more easily than smaller ones.

Adapted from Paul E. Rosene, "Musical Insights for the Exceptional Child," *Illinois Music Educator*, Fall 1987, 24-26.

* * *

Teaching Techniques

Teachers are always looking for ways to improve their effectiveness in the classroom. Sometimes this means trying out new activities or new ways to accomplish their goals; at other times it means being reminded of tools they have heard about but have forgotten. These TIPS focus on ways the teacher can bring efficiency, pleasure, and freshness to the music class.

Song stories, sometimes called sociodramas, minimusicals, or music dramas, all have a story line that links songs and activities with dialogue. The song story helps the child understand themes, moral points, or social activities. Many publishers carry song stories, but those you write will match the specific ability levels of your students. To write a song story, create a story line and write one or two simple, repeatable songs. Use much repetition, and try to include a strong social or moral objective. Try to keep song stories short so they can be performed in one class period. They can be presented at parents' meetings, special assemblies, or for other classes. Many special learners will remember songs and music activities if they have been attached to a story line. These music experiences will help motivate and encourage mainstreamed special learners in music classes.

Adapted from Paul E. Rosene, "Musical Insights for the Exceptional Child," *Illinois Music Educator*, Winter 1983, 31-33.

* * *

All people have creative potential; creativity and intelligence are not directly correlated. Teachers of special learners should not be afraid to encourage creative thinking processes, which produce ideas and attitudes. Since creativity involves both primary (right-hemisphere processing, or divergency) and secondary (left-hemisphere processing, or convergency) processes, it should be an integral aspect of arts education.

* * *

A work such as Johann Pachelbel's *Canon in D* lends itself to a variety of activities for special learners. Different levels of learning and musical competence can be accommodated using the following activities:

- Moving—conduct meter, use Kodály hand signals for motifs throughout the work, move directionally by phrases.
- Playing—play the repetitious eight-note theme (D-A-B-F#-G-D-G-A) on resonator bells or other melodic instruments.
- Creating—vary the rhythmic patterns for each measure after the motifs are learned, and create different countermelodies from diatonic scales that range from simple to quite complex.
- Listening—sing with the motifs using letters, numbers, syllables, pure vowels, or combinations of sounds; use visual representation of motifs to aid in focusing attention.
- Singing—sing notes, write counterpoint, or create words to fit the music.
- Naming—identify pitches, describe variations in the music, name the instruments, and make stylistic comparisons using different versions of the work.
- Relaxing—rest while the music is playing as background sound.
- Timing—use the recording as a timing device for completing assignments.
- Appreciating—learn to enjoy the composition aesthetically.

* * *

Children love to wear hats for dressing up or play acting. Have a collection of hats that students can wear for a variety of purposes: to fit the words of a song, to march in a parade, to pretend they are particular characters, or to help interpret a piece of music.

You can also wear a hat to represent a special time in class. Wear a different hat for instrument time, listening time, farewell time, no talking time, and so forth. Such nonverbal types of communication catch the interest and attention of the children.

* * *

Use Orff-Schulwerk techniques in your classroom. This approach emphasizes the "whole child" by developing the uniqueness of each individual. It provides the teacher with a large repertoire of expressive techniques and improvisational devices. Children with handicaps can find their own talents and creative potential and can interact with nonhandicapped children to make music. Everyone is viewed as an individual with distinct abilities.

Adapted from Suzanne B. Hanser, "The Orff-Schulwerk Approach," *California Music Educators Association News*, May-June 1985, 29.

* * *

Put up a solfege scale on the music room door, using appropriate patterns for each season. Some examples are September, schoolhouses; October, ghosts; November, Pilgrim hats; December, Christmas trees; January, snowflakes; February, hearts; March, shamrocks; April, raindrops; May, sunshine; and June, tennis shoes. Use these scales to teach solmization.

Adapted from Nancy Green and Janis Pauli, "Musigram," *Illinois Music Educator*, Spring 1987, 24.

* * *

Create a secret "pass song" (using three to five pitches or whatever is appropriate for each class) that the students have to sing before entering or leaving the room. Point to the syllable to be sung either by an individual or the entire class. If the intervals are sung correctly, the students can then pass through the door. Other variations could include having a student point to the syllables to be sung; giving point values for correctly sung syllables or intervals; adding rhythmic patterns to the correctly sung syllables or intervals; and having students make up their own "pass songs," notate the new composition, or play the new composition on tone bells or a keyboard.

Adapted from Nancy Green and Janis Pauli, "Musigram," *Illinois Music Educator*, Spring 1987, 24.

* * *

Create your own magnetic board by hinging together two metal stove-top protectors with a piano hinge or duct tape. Pictures, shapes, and music symbols can be backed with pieces of magnetic tape and stuck onto the board. Use these objects to give the students visual, tactile, and kinesthetic experiences as they manipulate the various symbols on the magnetic board. Seasonal pictures, pictures of instruments, colors, and shapes of all types can all be used for an interesting display.

* * *

If you are not adept at creating an original tune on the spot, use some familiar children's songs that have repeated rhythmic or melodic phrases and adapt the words to fit your needs. "Brother John," "Go Tell Aunt Rhody," "Twinkle, Twinkle Little Star," "The Farmer in the Dell," "London Bridge," "Happy Birthday," "Kum Ba Yah," and "Mary Had a Little Lamb" are all useful tunes. Since the children already know the tunes, they will have less trouble learning the new words you might use to teach names, telephone numbers, days of the week, colors, or other subjects.

* * *

Put both hands on your head without a word as a signal—the students should do the same. Then everyone sits down quietly, keeping hands on their heads until seated. (Students may find it easier to sit this way than teachers do.) Use the same cue and process for standing up. This is called sitting or standing "the magic way."

Writing individualized education programs (IEPs) should be an ongoing activity for all who teach music to exceptional students. Often the procedures are well stated and the resources are adequate, but the objectives are vague or nonexistent. All objectives must be clearly stated and possess three attributes that specify learner outcomes:

1. A verb denoting observable actions (behaviors)
2. The conditions under which the actions (behaviors) will take place
3. The desired level of achievement

These elements are essential to IEPs if the educator is to communicate what the student must do to achieve the objectives.

Adapted from "Paul E. Rosene, "Musical Insights for the Exceptional Child," *Illinois Music Educator*, Spring 1987, 34.

* * *

Keep accurate data as you work with your special learners. Take a few moments after private instructional sessions to record what occurred during the session. Recalling the events later is especially difficult for the typical music educator who has many students each day. Progress is easier to see if you keep accurate notes.

Adapted from Paul E. Rosene, "Musical Insights for the Exceptional Child," *Illinois Music Educator*, Winter 1987, 42.

* * *

Plan ahead for music lessons. Be flexible, however, and willing to learn from your students. Incorporate their feedback into your lessons. If a child is having a difficult time, offer him or her an opportunity to respond in a different way; for example, allow a hearing-impaired child to write or demonstrate the answer rather than speaking or signing it, or have a mentally retarded child play a simple two-note ostinato rather than a more complicated pattern.

This progress report has been used for trainable mentally handicapped students. It is easy to follow, and the parents have been satisfied with it.

Progress Evaluation

Name ______________ Instructor (Classroom) ____________

School ______________ Instructor (Other) ______________

Class ______________

	Needs Improving	Improving	Good
I. General attitude:			
A. Toward the class			
B. Toward the teacher and music			
II. Use of skills and concepts:			
A. Melody			
1. Participation in singing			
2. Use of pitches in singing			
3. Knowledge of pitches			
B. Rhythm and beat			
1. Use of instruments			
2. Use of body (to clap and stamp)			
3. Knowledge of rhythm and beat			
4. Recall of game or dance patterns			
C. Creativity			
1. Originality in arts			
2. Spontaneous reactions			
D. Group participation and cooperation			
1. Fair play in music, games, and dances			
2. Willingness to do activities			

Comments:____

Reprinted from Carol Guymer, "Special Spectrum," *North Dakota Music Educator*, October 1986, 25-26. Used with permission.

Refer to the MENC publication *Opportunity-to-Learn Standards for Music Instruction: Grades PreK–12* (1994) for specific recommendations about administrative support when a handicapped child is mainstreamed into music classes. These recommendations include active educator involvement in the initial placement of the child, placement based primarily on music achievement, provision of in-service or preservice training for teachers, convenient access to trained consultants in special education, and a general recommendation regarding adequate time for teacher preparation.

* * *

It is important to strike a balance between not expecting your students to do the impossible but challenging them to do all they are capable of doing. All children want to succeed, and they should have the opportunity to do so. Special learners need to know when they have done something well, have made an improvement, or have given a particular task a good try. Sometimes they need tangible rewards such as stickers or stars on a chart, but physical rewards such as a hug, a pat on the back, a squeeze of the hand, or verbal rewards (such as "Good job!" or "That sounded even better than the last one") are much more desirable. We need to emphasize the positives and not dwell on the negatives.

* * *

Students with special needs learn best in a structured setting that provides repetition and a familiar routine. Begin your music sessions with an established opening, and end with a familiar song that leads into the next activity. Plan a well-balanced music class with a wide array of activities. Activities involving considerable physical movement should be followed by calmer activities. Part of the session should be structured and require imitation, repetition, a specific song, or a steady beat. Allow time for freedom of exploration and improvisation in movement, rhythm, singing, and playing instruments. Plan activities that allow for both individual participation and group interaction. Change the activity before the onset of boredom or fatigue.

Adapted from Ruthlee Figlure Adler, *Target on Music* (Bethesda, MD: Christ Church Child Center, 1982), 4.

Movement games help motivate students and promote concentration, coordination, and creative activity. They also provide a release from tension between difficult academic tasks. These movements are examples; the children should create their own patterns, using their hands and arms. Practice this activity first with slow music, then increase the tempo as the children become more experienced.

Part 1 has sixteen beats; part 2 has thirty-two beats.

Part 1: Clap hands twice. Pat knees twice.
Pound fists twice, one atop the other. Reverse.
Pound fist into palm twice. Reverse.
Touch one elbow twice. Reverse.

Part 2: Swing an imaginary lasso overhead four times with one arm. Reverse. Move arms in a "hitchhike" motion (bending arm at the elbow and motioning outward with hand) four times.

"Cool wave" (hold hand with palm outward about a foot from waist and make circles) four times with one hand, then the other. Lock hands and swing hands over each shoulder twice on each side.

Catch a fly, put him in your hand, throw him on the ground, and stamp on him (catch, put, throw, stamp).

Adapted from Kay Hardesty, *Music for Special Education* (Morristown, NJ: Silver Burdett, 1979), 29

* * *

Music symbols (as well as letters, numbers, and various other shapes) can be cut from sandpaper and glued to cards or made with yarn dipped into white glue and molded to the desired shape. Students with visual handicaps, learning disabilities, and retarded students can benefit from using these cards.

* * *

Many times we need simple one- or two-chord accompaniments to songs so that the children can participate more easily in some form of accompanying. A list of some possible songs to use is helpful to keep on hand. Add your own ideas to this list:

One Chord	*Two Chords*	
Are You Sleeping? (Frère Jacques)	Blow the Man Down	Love Somebody
The Farmer in the Dell	Down in the Valley	Mary Had a Baby
Mister Frog Went A-Courtin'	Eency Weency Spider	Saturday Night
Roll Over	Hey, Ho, Nobody Home	Shoo Fly
Row, Row, Row Your Boat	Hey, Lidee	Six Little Ducks
Zum, Gali Gali	Hot Cross Bun	Skip to My Lou
Looby Loo	London Bridge	Ten Little Indians
	Tom Dooley	

* * *

Use the acronym "ATARI" to remember five suggestions that will help you begin working with special children.

A—Attitudes: Examine your own feelings, past experiences, and attitudes toward special children and how they might affect your teaching.

T—Talk to the most important person—the child. Find out how you can help the child and let him or her know you are there if you are needed.

A—Ask questions of professionals, other teachers, and parents. It is especially important in the area of behavior management to have a consistent approach.

R—Read about particular disabilities, a child's IEP, articles in professional journals, pamphlets from associations for disabilities, and textbooks.

I—Individualize: Look beyond disabilities to individual children and what they need to learn most effectively.

* * *

Selected Readings

Adler, Ruthlee Figlure. *Target on Music.* Bethesda, MD: Christ Church Child Center, 1982.

Birkenshaw, Lois. *Music for Fun, Music for Learning.* 3d ed. St. Louis: Magnamusic-Baton, 1982.

Bitcon, Carol Hampton. *Alike and Different: The Clinical and Educational Use of Orff-Schulwerk.* Santa Ana, CA: Rosha Press, 1976.

Elliot, Barbara. *Guide to the Selection of Musical Instruments with Respect to Physical Ability and Disability.* Philadelphia: LINC Resources, 1982.

Foster, Betty. *Training Songs for Special People, Set One.* Boulder, CO: Myklas Music Press, 1979.

Gadling, Donna, and Daniel Pokorny. *You've Got a Song: Selected Popular Songs with Sign Language Interpretation.* Silver Spring, MD: National Association of the Deaf, 1979.

Gadling, Donna C., Daniel H. Pokorny, and Lottie L. Riekenhof. *Lift Up Your Hands: Inspirational and Patriotic Songs in the Language of Signs.* Washington, DC: National Grange, 1976.

Graham, Richard M., and Alice Beer. *Teaching Music to the Exceptional Child.* Englewood Cliffs, NJ: Prentice-Hall, 1980.

Hardesty, Kay. *Music for Special Education.* Morristown, NJ: Silver Burdett, 1979.

Hill, Cherie. *Joy in Music with Special People! A Collection of Recipes for Group Music Activities.* Coral Gables, FL: Cherie Hill, 1978.

Music Educators National Conference. *The School Music Program: Description and Standards.* Reston, VA: MENC, 1986.

Nocera, Sona. *Reaching the Special Learner through Music.* Morristown, NJ: Silver Burdett, 1979.

Nordoff, Paul, and Clive Robbins. *Music Therapy in Special Education.* New York: John Day, 1971.

Robbins, Carol, and Clive Robbins. *Music for the Hearing Impaired and Other Special Groups: A Resource Manual and Curriculum Guide.* St. Louis: Magnamusic-Baton, 1980.

Schulberg, Cecilia. *The Music Therapy Sourcebook: A Collection of Activities Categorized and Analyzed.* New York: Human Sciences Press, 1981.

Slyoff, Martha. *Music for Special Education.* Fort Worth, TX: Harris Publishing.

Spanko, Jean. *Taming the Anthill.* Memphis, TN: Memphis Musicraft Publications, 1985.

Vernazza, Marcelle. *Music Plus: For the Young Child in Special Education.* St. Louis: Magnamusic-Baton, 1978.

Weaks, Donna Gadling. *Lift Up Your Hands.* Vol. 2, *Favorite Songs with Sign Language Interpretation.* Washington, DC: National Grange, 1980.

* * *

Acknowledgments

MENC gratefully acknowledges the following educators who contributed to this booklet:

Ruthlee Figlure Adler .... Maryland
Nigel J. Cross .... Florida
Jane Cryder .... Kansas
Alice-Ann Darrow .... Kansas
Kate Gfeller .... Iowa
Nancy Green .... Illinois
Gioia Grosso .... Florida
Carol Guymer .... North Dakota
Suzanne B. Hanser .... California
Kay Hardesty-Logan .... Pennsylvania
Jenni Harrison .... North Carolina
Arthur W. Harvey .... Kentucky
Mark Hebert .... Florida
S. Jeannette Hinds .... North Dakota
Jane Hughes .... Florida
L. Hadley Hunt .... Virginia
Mary-Hannah Klontz .... Kentucky
Betty Krebs .... Illinois
Marie H. Liebel .... Florida
Cak Marshall .... Pennsylvania
Jane McLaren .... Ontario
Joan Muckenhirn-Morton .... North Dakota

1092-1M-02/00